THE
TINY
PLANETS

THE TINY PLANETS

Asteroids of Our Solar System

DAVID C. KNIGHT

with 21 photographs and diagrams
William Morrow and Company
New York 1973

Knight, David C
    The tiny planets.

    SUMMARY: Discusses the origin, history, discovery,
physical nature, and present and future uses of the
asteroids, or minor planets.
    1. Planets, Minor—Juvenile literature.
[1. Planets, Minor] I. Title.
QB651.K55   523.4′4   72-12946
ISBN 0-688-20072-9
ISBN 0-688-30072-3 (lib. bdg.)

The author wishes to express
his thanks and appreciation
to Dr. Franklyn M. Branley,
retired Chairman
of the American Museum—
Hayden Planetarium,
New York,
for checking his manuscript
and illustrations.

CONTENTS

THE
TINY
PLANETS

1
INTRODUCING
THE
ASTEROIDS

The journey from Mars out to the huge planet Jupiter is a very long one. Between these two major planets of our solar system is a vast, ring-shaped gap of more than 340 million miles. The gap is not altogether empty, however. In this immense zone of interplanetary space are thousands of tiny planets, each a miniature world in itself, perpetually orbiting the sun. These diminutive heavenly bodies are the asteroids.

It often comes as a surprise to people to learn that, in addition to the nine major planets of the solar system, there are so many minor planets orbiting the sun. The asteroids do not receive much popular attention, because they are so small that they are difficult to see, even with a telescope. All are invisible to the naked eye with the occasional exception of one named Vesta. The largest, Ceres, is about 480 miles in diameter. Many others are between ten and fifteen miles across. A vast, perhaps countless, number are less than a mile in diameter. It has been said that if an average-sized mountain were uprooted from earth and tossed out into space, it might very well resemble a typical asteroid in size and shape.

The great majority of asteroids appear like far-distant stars when viewed through a telescope—that is, like small points of faint light. The term *asteroid* comes from the Greek and means "starlike." The synonym, *planetoid*, meaning "planetlike body," is preferred by many, but astonomers tend to call them simply the minor planets. Whatever name one chooses, the asteroids, being solid masses of matter revolving around the sun, have all the qualifications

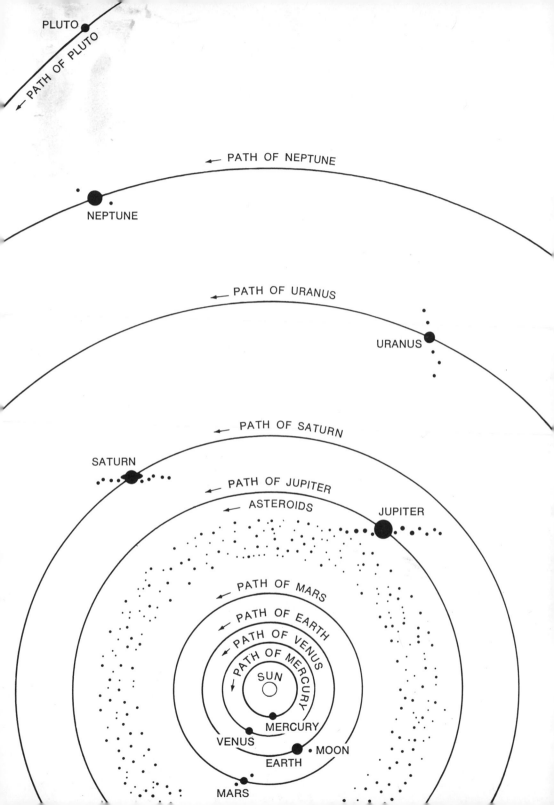

of true planets, except for their small size and ir-regular shape.

To date, more than 3000 asteroids have been dis-covered. Over 1650 of them have been assigned a number, and more than 1500 of them have proper names. Do astronomers know the total number of asteroids in our solar system? No, because the task of discovering, cataloging, and computing orbits for every asteroid large enough to be seen telescopically would be overwhelming. However, astronomers have made some educated guesses by systematically sampling selected regions of the sky. Using the 100-inch telescope, one astronomer photographed repre-sentative portions of the heavens and calculated that there must be at at least 44,000 minor planets within reach of the 100-inch instrument. More recently another astronomer obtained similar results. Probably no undiscovered asteroid of any size exists within the orbit of Mars, but in the zone beyond distant Jupiter, of course, a minor planet would have to be of great size to stand much chance of discovery.

Most asteroids travel uneventfully about the sun in paths that remain between the orbits of Mars and

Jupiter. Some of these flyweight worlds make the complete trip in one and a half years; others take up to six years; one takes over thirteen. A few, however, have quite unusual orbits that take them periodically out of the interplanetary zone between Mars and Jupiter. For example, Hermes travels in a nearly circular orbit, which centers on a point in space some distance away from the sun. At times Hermes

The orbit of an average asteroid contrasted with those that wander close to the sun.

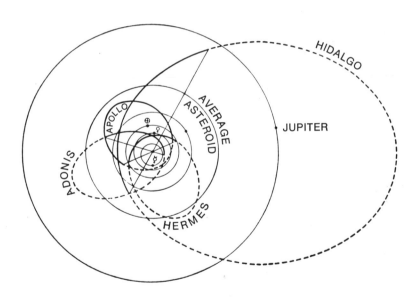

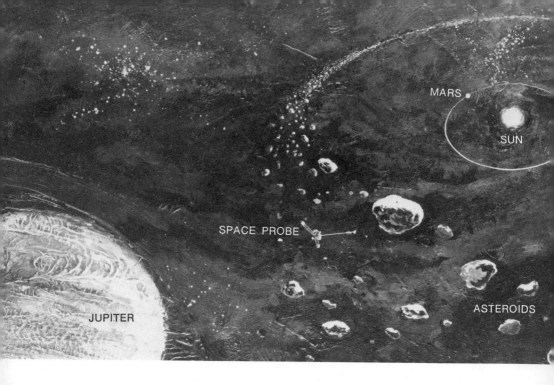

An artist's conception of an unmanned space probe over the surface of Jupiter showing a portion of the asteroid belt.

NASA

comes very close to the earth, passing once within 430,000 miles of it.

A few asteroids wander in quite close to the sun in long, cigar-shaped orbits. Because of their diminutive size and infrequent appearances, they rush across the sky so quickly that astronomers are aware of them only through the accident of discovery. No-

16

body really knows how many of these rocky objects may pass close to us each year without being detected. One, Icarus, moves in closer to the sun than the innermost planet, Mercury. Another, Hidalgo, moves far beyond the normal asteroid belt between Mars and Jupiter. It almost reaches the orbit of Saturn in its yearly journey. Still another asteroid with a peculiar, off-center orbit is Eros, which approaches so closely to earth that it may be, after the moon, the second heavenly body to be landed on by men.

According to modern custom, a newly discovered asteroid is given a name and number only after it has had its orbit calculated and it has been observed again after another completion of that orbit. This assigned number forms part of a running index indicating the order of its discovery among the minor planets. The usual designation of an asteroid contains both number and name, with the number circled and preceding the name, thus: ① Ceres, ② Pallas, ④ Vesta, and so on.

Just where the asteroids came from or how they were formed, no one as yet knows. Whatever their origin may have been, they are as permanent a part of our solar system as Venus, Neptune, or our own earth. Yet it was only a scant 175 years ago that the first asteroid was discovered. That discovery—and indeed the entire history of the minor planets—constitutes one of the most interesting chapters in the history of astronomy.

2
DISCOVERY
AND
HISTORY

As early as 1595, the German astronomer Johannes Kepler worked out a system for figuring the approximate distances from the sun of the six planets that were then known. There seemed to be a logical mathematical relationship between them. However, Kepler and his fellow astronomers noticed that a large gap of many millions of miles existed between the orbits of Mars and Jupiter. Kepler, a logical yet somewhat mystical man, was sure that a seventh, smaller and as yet undiscovered, planet belonged in this gap. To the end of his days, this irregularity puzzled Kepler—as it was to puzzle later astronomers —and he once wrote: "Between Mars and Jupiter, I interpose a planet."

Until the first asteroid discoveries, astronomers continued to believe that somewhere in this wide belt of the solar system there was a missing planet. This belief was fed and nourished in the 1770's by the discovery of a curious mathematical relationship known as Bode's Law, which is a helpful scheme for remembering the distances of the planets from the sun.

Actually Bode's Law was neither a law nor was it discovered by Bode. In 1772, J. D. Titius, a professor at the University of Wittenberg in Germany, had published a mathematical relationship that suggested the approximate numerical distances of the planets from the sun. Professor Titius's "law" probably would have been forgotten had it not come to the attention of Johann Bode, editor of the influential *Astronomical Yearbook* and director of the Berlin Observatory. Bode gave Titius's "law" such a great deal of publicity that in time it became known by his own name.

Bode's Law is very easy to understand. It is based on the series of numbers: 0, 3, 6, 12, 24, 48, and so on. Except for the zero at the beginning, each number in this progression is found by doubling the preceding number. When four is added to each of these numbers and the sums are divided by ten, the following series results: .4, .7, 1., 1.6, 2.8, 5.2, and so on.

The fascinating thing about the Law is that these figures are approximately equal to the average distances of most of the planets from the sun, as expressed in astronomical units. Astronomical units are used as a simple way of expressing distances within the solar system. One astronomical unit equals the distance in miles from the earth to the sun, or 93 million miles. Two astronomical units would be twice that distance, and so on.

The table on page 22 shows the amazingly close correspondence btween the figures yielded by the Bode-Titius rule and the actual distances of most of the planets from the sun.

Planet	Distance from Sun in Astronomical Units	Bode's Law
Mercury	0.4	0.4
Venus	0.7	0.7
Earth	1.0	1.0
Mars	1.52	1.6
?	?	2.8
Jupiter	5.2	5.2
Saturn	9.5	10.0
Uranus	19.2	19.6
Neptune	30.1	38.8
Pluto	39.5	77.2

It can be seen that Bode's Law works perfectly well up to, and including, the distance for Uranus. When, in 1781, Sir William Herschel discovered that planet, its distance of 19.2 astronomical units fitted in reasonably well with the Law, which had predicted that a new planet would be found at about that distance from the sun. The Law obviously breaks down completely in the case of Neptune, discovered in 1846, and Pluto, discovered in 1930, so that after the mid-nineteenth century faith in the Bode-Titius relationship was badly shaken.

But, in 1801, Neptune and Pluto had not been found yet, and Bode's Law was regarded by many as a fundamental relationship. Up to that time, however, no planet had been found to correspond with the unoccupied distance of 2.8 units.

Johann Bode became convinced that there must be a missing planet somewhere at the unfilled position. And Bode, who was an influential man, convinced others. Thus, near the end of the eighteenth century, an association of twenty-four German astronomers banded together to locate the unknown planet. Knowing that they would have to search systematically the region of the sky called the Zodiac, they divided it up into twenty-four equal areas—one for each observer—and began their quest.

As matters turned out, these men might have saved themselves the trouble, for on January 1, 1801, in Palermo, Sicily, a fifty-four-year-old Italian priest named Giuseppi Piazzi made an amazing discovery. A director of the Palermo Observatory, he had turned his attention to a certain region of the sky in the constellation Taurus because of an error in a star catalog. Piazzi meant to remap this particular area and correct the error. On this, the first night of the new century, the sky was clear and observation was excellent.

Piazzi was soon surprised to notice through his telescope a starlike object that he had difficulty in identifying in the catalogs. It was of about the seventh magnitude—that is, not quite bright enough to be seen without the aid of a telescope. He was puzzled, for the object was in a position in the heavens where no such body of that magnitude should have been. Furthermore, it seemed slowly to change its position among the stars.

The next night he observed the object again. Its position apparently had shifted slightly eastward. On January 3, he was sure that it was moving. Piazzi was now certain that the object could not possibly be a "star," that is, a distant sun. Such rapid movement of a celestial body against the backdrop of unchanging stars meant that it had to be comparatively close to earth. In other words, it was probably a member of our solar system, as were comets and the planets.

Father Piazzi became convinced that he had discovered a new comet. But it had neither a tail nor the characteristic fuzziness of most comets. Still, it was quite far from the sun, where most comets usually develop a tail and a blurred appearance around their head.

Piazzi followed the mysterious object for several more nights. There could be no question that it was moving. He made several observations of it, so that an orbit, or path, could be calculated for it.

During this time the "comet" had been traveling in an easterly direction among the stars. Then, in mid-January, the monk was startled to see it stop and start moving in a westerly direction. Such a reversal, or retrograde motion, of an object in the sky had been known from ancient times. The Greeks called such objects *planets* (meaning "wanderers") because of their zigzag motion first in one direction, then another. This same looping motion had led early astronomers to think that the planets moved in very complex circular movements around the earth.

As an educated man, Father Piazzi was well aware that this looping motion of the planets was merely an illusion due to the fact that the earth is also revolving around the sun. The earth regularly overtakes planets farther away from the sun and is itself being overtaken by Venus and Mercury, which are nearer the sun. The nearer a planet is to the sun, the shorter its orbit, and so it completes its orbits more often than the outlying planets.

Piazzi went on observing the object for the rest of January. As the days went by, he gradually came to the conclusion that it was not a comet at all, but a new small planet. Eventually Father Piazzi named the tiny planet Ceres, after the Roman goddess protector of Sicily.

Then, about February 11, Piazzi became ill and could observe his new planet no longer. When he was well enough to return to his telescope, Ceres had become lost below the horizon.

Even so, Father Piazzi had managed to make some good observations of the object, and he had written to some German astronomers about his discovery. He had asked, moreover, for their help in calculating an orbit for Ceres, so that it could be rediscovered at a later date. The trouble was that he had watched the new little planet for only six short weeks. No orbit

The path of Ceres (arrow) as it was viewed by Piazzi from January 1 to its disappearance on February 11. The word ecliptic here refers to the path of the sun among the stars during a year's time. Piazzi observed the phenomenon on the successive dates shown.

Courtesy of the American Museum of Natural History

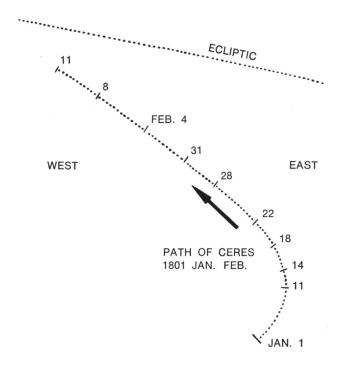

ever had been successfully computed from observations extending over such a brief period.

A young German mathematician, Karl Friedrich Gauss, came to the rescue. Gauss, then teaching at the University of Göttingen, had devised a simplified method for calculating the orbit of a heavenly body from only three observations. Using Piazzi's charts, he figured out the orbit of Ceres and by November, 1801, announced the approximate spot in the heavens where the object could be rediscovered. Unfortunately, the weather turned cloudy for a few weeks. Then on the last night of the year, December 31, 1801, Baron Franz Xavier von Zach, a German astronomer, located Ceres in the constellation Virgo. The very next night—exactly one year after Father Piazzi's discovery—an amateur astronomer, a German physician named Heinrich W. M. Olbers, also observed Ceres. The tiny planet was very near the spot where Gauss had said it would be.

Von Zach, Olbers, Gauss, and other investigators all realized that Giuseppe Piazzi had made a great discovery—not merely because he had been the first man to observe a new heavenly object, but because of its special location in the solar system. Ceres was just about 2.8 astronomical units away from the sun. Thus, astronomers believed that Father Piazzi finally had discovered the elusive "missing planet."

Then a still more surprising find was made. One night in March, 1802, Heinrich Olbers sighted another small planet. Olbers had been hunting for comets, and his discovery was accidental. Gauss calculated the orbit and found that this body, too, moved between Mars and Jupiter at about the same distance as Ceres—2.8 units from the sun. It was named Pallas. Today it is known to be the second largest asteroid, with a diameter of 304 miles.

In 1804, a third small planet was discovered by an astronomer named Karl Harding. Called Juno, it had a diameter of about 120 miles; it is the fourth largest of the asteroids.

Vesta, the third largest of the minor planets, with a diameter of 240 miles, was discovered by Doctor Olbers in 1807. Olbers had observed that the orbits of the first three asteroids crossed each other in the constellation Virgo. Thinking that they might be the surviving fragments of a shattered planet, he was searching for other fragments when he found Vesta.

Then, for thirty-eight long years, no further asteroids were identified. True, laborious searches were conducted for new ones, but the searchers were unsuccessful because they did not look for sufficiently faint objects.

As the years passed, astronomers began to think that there were only four of these tiny planets. Still, about the year 1830, another amateur astronomer named Karl Hencke, who lived in Berlin, began hunting for a fifth. After fifteen years he finally found it in 1845 and named it Astrea. Encouraged, he kept on with his search and after two more years found a sixth, which he named Hebe.

Other astronomers joined the investigation. Two more asteroids were found in 1847—Iris and Flora—numbers 7 and 8. Number 9 was named Metis; number 10, Hygeia; number 11, Parthenope; number 12, Victoria; and number 13 was called Egeria. Then, exactly half a century after Piazzi discovered Ceres, number 14 was found and named Irene.

During the next twenty years, from 1850 to 1870, an average of five new minor planets were discovered every year. The discoverers followed the tradition of giving them female classical names, but soon they were in short supply. Nymphs and goddesses were rapidly consumed; so were the nine muses and female characters from the *Odyssey*. Number 18 was named Melpomene; number 26, Proserpine; number 29, Amphitrite; number 53, Kalypso (spelled with a "k" in literal translation from the Greek); number 85, Io; number 179, Klytemnestra; number 195, Eurycleia; and so on.

By the year 1890, there were some 300 known asteroids, and the classical lexicon had long since yielded up most of its female names to become enshrined in the sky as asteroids. For a while discoverers were content to name their tiny planets after German and Wagnerian heroines. For example, number 165 was called Lorelei and number 242, Kriemhild. Then countries were resorted to, with number 232 becoming Russia and 241, Germania.

Up till 1890, the methods of astronomical observation were quite laborious. There were as yet no photographic atlases showing faint stars, let alone a faint starry object like an asteroid. First an asteroid hunter had to plot the area of the sky that he was interested in, then replot the same area at a later time, and finally compare the two charts to see if there were any revealing changes. At that time, however, Professor Max Wolf, of Heidelberg, began using photographic plates to observe and make a permanent record of the heavens. Thus the present-day technique of celestial photography was born. Faint objects, such as asteroids, no longer needed to be patiently hunted down by eye and hand, but could quite literally be "trapped" in a photographic net.

The new method was, in principle, rather simple. A telescope with a camera attached was focused on a particular area of the sky for two or three hours. To the apparatus was added a very slow driving clock, which allowed the telescope and camera to keep up with the distant stars as the earth rotated and they shifted in the heavens. On the exposed photographic plate, the stars appeared as solid points or round dots, because the camera was keeping up with their apparent movement. But if an asteroid, moving much faster within the solar system against the "fixed" stars, was present in that area of the sky, it showed up as a short dash or streak on the resulting photograph. The first asteroid to betray its existence photographically was Brucia, number 323.

From that time on, the exciting days of asteroid hunting were over, and a new era of constant discovery began. The first twenty or so asteroids had brought their finders high honors; the next three hundred were still good for astronomical recognition;

The trail of an asteroid. Behind it, the distant stars appear as solid dots on the exposed photographic plate.

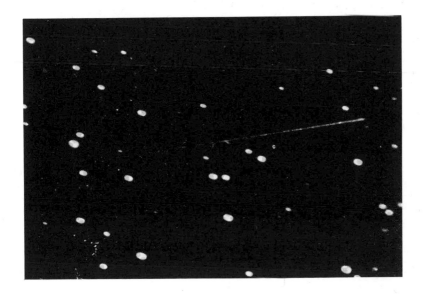

afterward the location of an asteroid became routine. In the half century from 1890 to 1940, the number of legitimate, recognized asteroids increased from three hundred to almost fifteen hundred. Nevertheless, important astronomical events resulted. For example, after Wolf's new photographic method was introduced, the Germans established a Computing Institute for Minor Planets, a sort of world clearinghouse into which the rest of the astronomical community siphoned its observations.

But soon so many asteroids were being discovered that scientists began to complain about the "minor planets' plague." One American astronomer even referred to the plethora of newly discovered asteroids as "vermin of the skies." Indeed, all too often serious-minded astronomers, perhaps searching for a new comet or some other phenomenon, would find their photographic plates spotted with the tracks of asteroids.

Nevertheless, on August 13, 1898, Dr. G. Witt of the Urania Observatory in Berlin found something exceptional on one of his plates. It was obviously another asteroid, but one with a difference. The

34

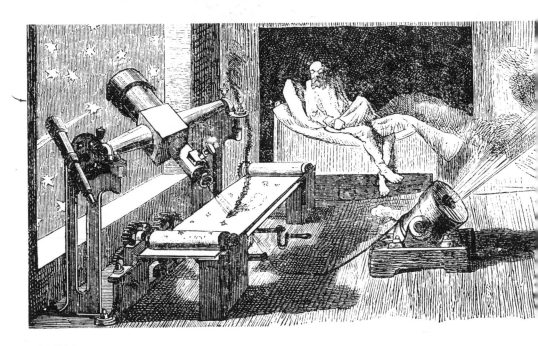

A nineteenth-century German cartoon shows how common the discovery of asteroids had become. The astronomer does not bother to get out of bed as a cannon, attached to his telescope, announces another discovery. The original caption pointed out that a salvo could be expected every fifteen minutes because the possible number of asteroids between Mars and Jupiter was so vast.

short telltale dash on the plate was unusually long, meaning that the asteroid was traveling very rapidly. It also meant that it was quite near the earth. An orbit was calculated for it, the number 433 assigned, and the object was named Eros after the Greek god of love. It was the first masculine name to be assigned an asteroid.

Eros's importance was recognized early. It was calculated that Eros's year, or *period*, was 643 days and that its closest approach to the sun, called *perihelion*, was only 1.13 astronomical units—nearly that of earth's. The orbits and periods of Eros and earth were found to work out in such a way that Eros would come quite close to earth—about fourteen million miles—roughly every forty years. Unfortunately for Witt and his colleagues, the closest possible approach that would occur in their own lifetimes *already* had taken place four years earlier, in 1894. A later search through old photographic plates at Harvard Observatory for that year revealed that Eros had been photographed accidentally over a dozen times without being officially discovered. In 1931, Eros approached the earth at a distance of some sixteen million miles. Its next such appearance will be in January, 1975.

The discovery of new asteroids continued. Num-

ber 443 was named Photographica, obviously honoring Max Wolf's contribution to astronomy. (Wolf himself was credited with some 587 discoveries, and his colleague, Karl Reinmuth, at the same observatory, was credited with 980 up to 1941. However, no orbits were computed for many of these objects; perhaps one or two observations were made and then the object was lost. Some may have been rediscovered later by another astronomer.)

Then, in 1908, Max Wolf himself discovered the next unusual asteroid. It was number 588, and it seemed to be moving in the same orbit that the huge planet Jupiter traveled in. Achilles, as it was named, turned out to be rather large for an asteroid—its diameter was later estimated to be 150 miles—and it was the first to be discovered of an important group of asteroids all named after heroes of the Trojan War. They make up the group known as the "Trojan family."

Meanwhile, the finding of additional minor planets went on. Cities were honored: number 325 was named Heidelbergia; number 484, Pittsburghia. Scientists were honored: number 855 was named Newcombia, after Simon Newcomb; number 1002 became Olbersia, after Olbers. Colleges and universities came in for their share of recognition: number 736 was named Harvardia; number 1312, Vassar. Number 694 was called Ekard, which is Drake (University) spelled backwards. Number 671 was called Carnegia, obviously by someone who admired either Andrew Carnegie or his Institute. After World War I, a Russian astronomer named an asteroid Ara, not after the constellation of that name, but after the initials of the American Relief Administration, which saved the lives of many starving Russians with food contributions.

In 1920, the well-known Swiss astronomer, Dr. Walter F. Baade, discovered the important asteroid, Hidalgo, meaning "Spanish nobleman," which has a period of nearly fourteen of our own earth years—the longest of any known minor planet. In 1932, Karl Reinmuth found a rapidly moving asteroid whose orbit brings it close to earth and named it Apollo. Nearly four years later, in 1936, the Belgian astronomer, E. Delaporte, detected another closely approaching asteroid that he named Adonis. The following year Reinmuth found Hermes, a tiny planet with an orbit that at its minimum distance from the earth was no more than twice the distance of our own planet from the moon. Apollo, Hermes, and Adonis all travel in orbits that cross within that of Venus, and all are estimated to be about a mile in diameter.

A slightly smaller asteroid was discovered by Walter Baade in June, 1949. Baade called it Icarus, after the mythical boy whose wax wings melted when he flew too close to the sun. It was detected by Baade on a photograph taken with the forty-eight-inch Schmidt telescope at Mount Palomar in California. At its perihelion, closest approach to the sun, Icarus passes within seventeen million miles of the sun. It then sweeps out far beyond the orbit of Mars, but returns to perihelion after only 409 days—a little longer than an earth year.

Icarus is moving very rapidly in its orbital path. So are the other closely approaching asteroids: Adonis, Apollo, Hermes, and Eros. All were discovered by accident, a fact that illustrates how easily a mountain-sized mass of rock can hurtle past the earth at super-

The trail (at arrow) of the asteroid Icarus photographed in June, 1949, the month of its discovery by Walter Baade. Photograph was taken with the 48-inch Schmidt telescope.
Mount Wilson and Palomar Observatories

high speeds without observation. The asteroids Apollo, Adonis, and Hermes have not, in fact, been seen again since their original near-approach to earth during the 1930's. These three asteroids received no official numbers at the time of their discovery because World War II was imminent in Europe and all numbering was discontinued for the duration of the conflict.

During this period, newspaper stories began to appear about what would happen if an asteroid collided with the earth. It is not beyond the bound of possibility that someday one of these undetected flying objects might pass perilously close to the earth, or even score a direct hit. If such an event ever occurred—say, with a body a mile or so in diameter—it would devastate an enormous area and send shock waves to every part of our planet. To date, however, there is no certain proof that the earth has ever been hit by a body the size of Icarus or larger. The famous meteor crater in Arizona is thought to have been produced by a large meteroid or a small comet, but such an object would have been much smaller than any of the asteroids whose orbits are known. In any case, most astronomers believe that the chance of a collision with one of these tiny planets is so mathematically remote that they are not seriously concerned about the possibility.

Today, discoveries of asteroids are usually accidental, for astronomers are not particularly on the lookout for them. They occur most often when these tiny planets leave their tracks on photographs taken for other astronomical purposes. Indeed, when a modern astronomer sees on his plate an elongated image that is presumably an asteroid, he seldom bothers to pursue the matter further—unless the streak is an exceptionally long one, indicating an object moving near the arth. Literally thousands of such streaks are found on plates at modern observatories,

A photograph of the light trails of two asteroids. One appears at left center, the other at top right.

and the majority of them never have been cataloged. Most, in fact, have been ignored because at least three (and preferably more) observations are required, separated by several weeks, before an official orbit can be determined.

But despite the huge number of these seemingly insignificant worlds, the orbital motions of a few of them fascinate astronomers—and render at least some of the tiny planets useful to mankind.

3
PHYSICAL NATURE

The asteroids of the solar system all revolve about the sun in the same direction as the major planets do; that is, counterclockwise, as viewed by an observer out in space. And, like the nine planets, the asteroids all make their yearly orbital journeys in geometrically curved paths called *ellipses*.

Knowing what an ellipse is is most important to understanding the motions of any heavenly body in the solar system. Why? Because nearly all bodies in interplanetary space move in such curves. No known natural body that is a member of the solar system orbits the sun in a perfect *circle*, which is defined as a closed curve, every point of which is equally distant from a point within it called the center.

The difference between a circle and an ellipse is shown in the accompanying diagram of two cones, sliced at different angles. If a cone—a solid body tapering evenly to a point from a circular base—is cut anywhere parallel to its base, a circle is made at the cutoff surface. If the same cone is sliced through at an angle to its base, however, the figure made at the cutoff surface is an ellipse.

While a circle has only one focus point, or center, an ellipse has two. The foci of an ellipse always lie on its principal axis, an imaginary line drawn through the center of the figure. The two foci are equidistant from the center point of that axis. Their distance from the circumference determines the shape of the curve. The foci of an ellipse are very important, because when a body such as a planet or an asteroid is in orbital motion, the sun, with its huge gravitational force, is always at one focus of the

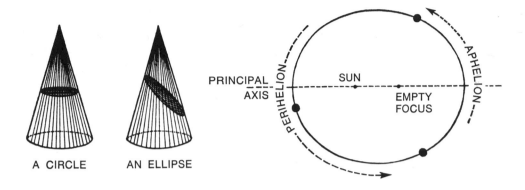

Left: Conic sections show difference between a circle and an ellipse. *Right:* An elliptical orbit showing foci.

elliptical orbit; the other focus is sometimes referred to as an empty focus.

The asteroids in the main belt between Mars and Jupiter journey about the sun in ellipses that are more or less circular. But a few minor planets orbit the sun in long, flattened, cigar-shaped ellipses that astronomers call *highly eccentric.* Eccentricity means how much an ellipse is flattened, or squashed, and is indicated by values ranging from 0 to 1. An orbit with zero eccentricity would be a perfect circle; the more eccentric an orbit is, the more closely it approaches 1.

A few comparisions with the major planets show how eccentric some of the asteroids' orbits are. The eccentricity of seven of the nine planetary orbits is less than 0.1 Earth's is a mere 0.017, that is, quite circular. Mercury's is 0.2. Pluto's is the most eccentric at 0.25. While the average eccentricity for the asteroids is only 0.15, about seven percent of the minor planets have eccentricities greater than Pluto's.

In most cases, an asteroid with a very eccentric orbit is also inclined to the earth's orbit at a very steep angle, although this relationship is not always so. Astronomers use the plane of the earth's orbit as

The asteroid Icarus is inclined 21 degrees to the earth's orbit.

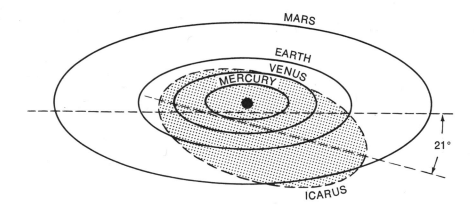

a standard against which to compare the tilt, or slant, of other planetary orbits. As shown in the diagram, Icarus's orbit is inclined twenty-one degrees to that of the earth's. The asteroid whose orbit is tilted the most to earth's is Betulia—a huge fifty-two degrees. Before Betulia's orbit was known, the asteroid thought to have the greatest inclination to earth's was Hidalgo, with forty-three degrees.

Largely because of their high eccentricity, a few asteroids—those in the seven percent mentioned— do not remain in the main asteroid zone between Mars and Jupiter, but wander in close to earth's orbit and the sun itself. One of these is Icarus, which has the smallest orbit among the asteroids. It comes within some four million miles of the earth at times and penetrates to seventeen million miles of the sun. As can be seen in the diagram on page 50, Hidalgo is the asteroid with the largest orbit. It travels further from the sun than any other known minor planet. At *aphelion*, the point in its orbit farthest from the sun, it swings out nearly to the orbit of Saturn, and at perihelion it passes a point just beyond the orbit of Mars.

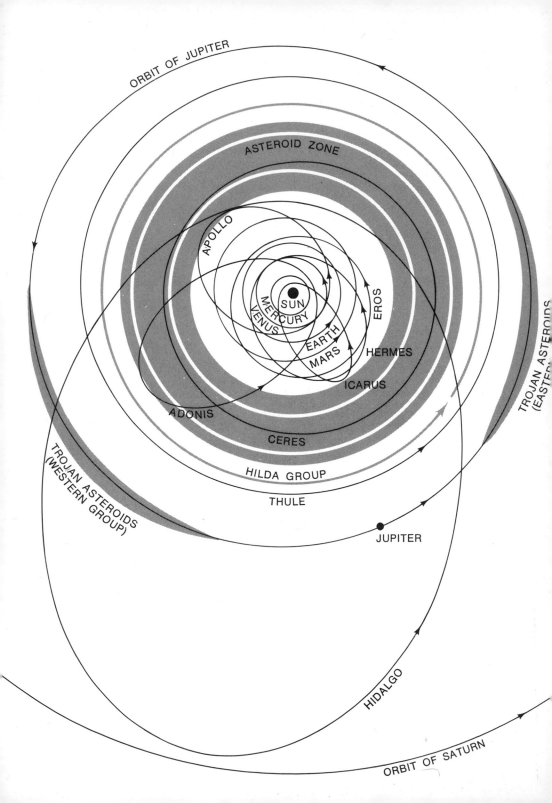

The diagram also shows other highly eccentric asteroids that pass close to earth's orbit and the sun. One of these is Eros. Another, Apollo, comes within the orbit of Venus and passes the earth at two points less than three million miles away. Adonis skirts the earth at about one million miles, passes Venus and Mars at approximately the same distance, and gets within some five million miles of Mercury's orbit. Hermes, at the time of its discovery, was only about 600,000 miles away from the earth.

Actually the asteroid with the most accurately computed, *known* orbit that gets closest to earth is Icarus. In a sense, it is "in captivity," for its return to earth can be calculated with great precision. In June, 1968, it passed within about four million miles of the earth—right on the schedule that astronomers had predicted. Geographos is another asteroid whose orbit is well known. It passed within some six million miles of the earth in 1969—also on schedule.

Some of the asteroids take only about one and a half years to make their complete revolution around the sun. Others take as long as five or six earth years to do so. Hidalgo, with its highly eccentric orbit and steep inclination, takes over thirteen and a half years to make one complete circuit of the sun.

Astronomers refer to the highly eccentric orbits of such asteroids as Icarus, Hermes, Hidalgo, and others as *cometary orbits*. This term is used because their paths resemble the elongated, flat elliptical orbits of our solar system's comets. In fact, such eccentric minor planets and comets may be related, for some scientists have speculated that, for instance, Hidalgo might really be the remains of a comet whose *coma*, the glowing part of its head, has long since disappeared.

One interesting thing about the distribution of the asteroids is the existence of a number of empty spaces or gaps in the main zone between Mars and Jupiter. They are known as *Kirkwood's gaps*, because they were explained first by Daniel Kirkwood, in 1866, as being due to perturbations caused by the giant planet Jupiter. Astronomers say that a heavenly body is *perturbed*, or deviated, from its orbit when it is attracted by another celestial body or bodies. These gaps in the asteroid belt can be seen in the accompanying diagram.

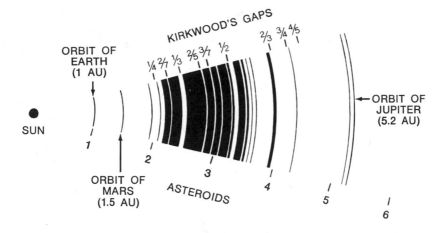

Kirkwood's gaps in the asteroid belt are shown in fractions of Jupiter's period (above). Distance from the sun in astronomical units indicated by numerals (below).

Courtesy of the American Museum of Natural History

Astronomers still cannot explain why these gaps occur where they do in the otherwise thickly populated asteroid zone. What they *do* know is that the gaps occur at distances from the sun that correspond to simple fractions of Jupiter's period of nearly twelve earth years. Specifically, the gaps are present at distances that are mathematically equivalent to ½, ⅖, ⅔, etc., of the big planet's period. Scientists believe that the immense gravitational pull of Jupiter builds up at these points in the asteroid belt and somehow sweeps these areas clear of minor planets.

Besides the absence of asteroids in the mysterious gaps, there are also concentrations in unusual numbers that form asteroid groups or "families." By far the most important of these clusters is the Trojan group. All the members of this group are named after such heroes of the Trojan War as Priam, Patroclus, Ajax, Hector, Achilles, and others.

The story of how the Trojan group came to be recognized as a family is an interesting one. In 1772, the French mathematician Joseph Lagrange worked out one solution to a classic problem in *celestial mechanics*, the branch of astronomy that deals with the motions of celestial bodies under the forces of gravitation. This problem was the so-called "three body problem." It posed the question of how three bodies traveling fairly close together in space would affect each others' motion.

Lagrange's work suggested to later astronomers that there might be two points—now called Lagrangian points—on the orbit of Jupiter at or near which a hypothetical asteroid could remain almost indefinitely. Specifically, Lagrange's mathematics implied that when the three bodies formed an equilateral triangle—an equal-sided triangle with each

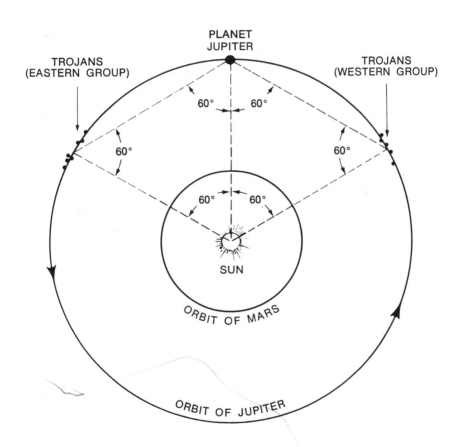

angle being sixty degrees—they would be locked in a stable system. Three such bodies could possibly be Jupiter, the sun, and one or more asteroids on either side of Jupiter, as shown in the diagram.

When Max Wolf discovered Achilles in 1904, the asteroid's position was seen to fit into this scheme. Achilles travels at the same distance from the sun as Jupiter but about sixty degrees ahead of the big planet, thus forming two angles of an equilateral triangle with the sun. By 1908, four more such asteroids had been discovered. In 1959, the number increased to fourteen. Some of these asteroids were found to form another group traveling sixty degrees *behind* Jupiter, forming another equilateral triangle with the sun.

Interestingly, over the years of their discovery the tradition has been to name the asteroids of the eastern (or leading) group after Greek warriors and those of the western (or trailing) group after Trojans. Unfortunately, this custom was established only after the first three asteroids had been named, with the result that there is one Greek "spy" among the western group and one Trojan "spy" among the eastern group. At present, there are five known asteroids in the western (or Trojan) side and nine in the eastern (or Greek) group.

While the Trojans circle the sun with Jupiter once every twelve years, one group ahead of it and one group behind, their actual motion in orbit is very complicated; they wobble slightly about their Lagrangian points. Part of the wobble is due to the perturbing influence of nearby Jupiter and part to that of Saturn.

Astronomers think that possibly some of Jupiter's twelve satellites, or moons, may once have been Trojan asteroids, and that they came too close to the huge planet and were captured by it. Likewise, some of the present Trojans may one day succeed in escaping their fixed position in the Jovian triangle and free themselves. Other asteroids may someday wander in too near to Jupiter and become captured as new Trojans. At the relatively great distance of Jupiter from the earth, only asteroids of fairly large size can be detected from our planet. Thus, there may be smaller members of the Trojan group too faint to have been discovered.

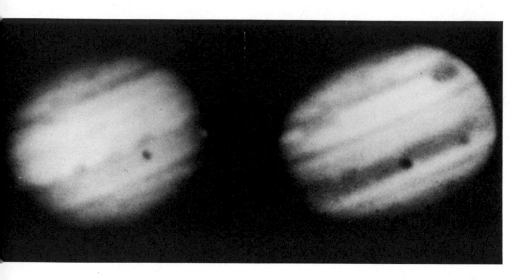

Two photographs of the planet Jupiter. A satellite and its shadow can be seen on both. The photo at right shows the Great Red Spot on the planet's surface. *Yerkes Observatory*

Astronomers are also quite certain that the minor planets, besides orbiting the sun, rotate on their axes as well. Some appear to be doing so faster than others. But even using powerful telescopes, how can astronomers be sure of this motion when they are dealing with such tiny bodies so far from earth? At present— until robot space probes or human beings can take motion pictures of them—scientists must determine an asteroid's rotational period by the amount of light it reflects, or its brightness.

Like all heavenly bodies in the solar system, the asteroids receive light from the sun. This light reflects—bounces off—an asteroid's surface and can be seen by scientists on earth. A few of the minor planets shine with a steadily reflected sunlight, but most keep changing in their level of brightness. For a brief period they look fairly bright; then they grow much dimmer.

Astronomers believe the explanation for this changing brightness lies in the asteroids' having irregular shapes instead of being spherical like the major planets. Probably most asteroids are craggy chunks of rocky material. When such an asteroid rotates on its axis, the smoother parts of its spinning surface reflect more sunlight back to earth than others. When sunlight strikes a pitted, rocky portion of the asteroid's surface, the rays break up and are reduced in strength. Thus an asteroid that shines with a steady light probably has a more rounded spherical shape, because it reflects an even amount of light from every part of its surface.

Scientists are able to study such light changes coming from the asteroids with a *photometer*, an instrument designed to register the intensity of light. By carefully observing and timing the bright and dim areas as they appear and disappear, they can calculate how fast the asteroid is rotating.

The amount of light an asteroid reflects is also used to measure its approximate size. In fact, the only way that the diameters of most asteroids can be estimated is by recording their brightness when they are at known distances from the earth and sun. Since most asteroids are too small to show a visible face, scientists can estimate their diameters from their brightness alone by guessing at a reasonable *albedo* for them. Albedo is the term for the reflecting power of a celestial body—the percentage of light it is capable of reflecting from its surface, as against the amount that is absorbed by it. For example, the moon reflects only seven percent of the sunlight it receives. The other ninety-three percent is absorbed by the lunar surface.

But how can astronomers guess at the albedos of such tiny bodies so far out in space? They do so by basing their guess on the "big four" asteroids—Pallas, Vesta, Ceres, and Juno. The albedos of these large asteroids can be calculated because their faces are big enough to be measured directly. Once the diameter is known, astronomers can calculate how much sunlight is falling upon the asteroid's surface and approximately how much is being reflected back to earth. The albedos of the "big four" have been found to average about 0.1; that is, they reflect about ten percent of the sunlight falling upon them. Astronomers assume that other minor planets have albedos of similar reflective power and are thus able to calculate roughly the sizes the asteroids must be to account for their observed brightness.

Diameters of asteroids estimated by this indirect method have been found to be as small as half a mile, and there may be asteroids that are far smaller. Indeed, the number of small rocky fragments in orbit about the sun may well be uncountable. In general, however, this indirect method of measuring asteroids by their brightness has indicated that, in addition to the "big four," there are probably about a dozen with diameters greater than one hundred miles. And there may be a few hundred that are more than twenty-five miles across. Most of the rest of the observable asteroids must have diameters of about a mile or so.

Using this indirect technique as early as 1901, astronomers studied the asteroid Eros and observed that its brightness varied sharply during its day of five hours and sixteen minutes. The only way they could explain the variations in brightness was with the theory that the asteroid must be shaped something like a brick. No one was sure of this explanation, however, until Eros made a close pass by the earth in 1931. So close did it come that astronomers were able to observe the asteroid telescopically, and its elongated, bricklike shape was confirmed. Eros is probably a world some fifteen to twenty miles long and about five miles wide and thick. Several other asteroids exhibit similar changes in brightness over periods of a few hours and are also assumed to be irregular in shape.

Most observable minor planets have rotational periods, days, of only a few hours. Some have days of only two or three hours; those of others are between five and eight hours; only a handful have a day even approaching that of earth's twenty-four hours. Thus a hypothetical man sitting in one spot on the small asteroid Florentina, which has a rotational period of about three hours, would witness some eight sunrises in the space of one of our own earth days.

Small as they may be compared to the major planets, the asteroids are still composed of rocky material that has measurable density and mass. *Density* means the *amount* of matter in a unit volume of a substance, while *mass* is the total *quantity* of matter that an entire body contains. Although both weight and mass are described in terms of pounds, tons, grams, or other weight units, mass is not the same as weight. Weight on the earth is the measure of the gravitational attraction of the earth for a body on or near its surface. The nearer the body is to the center of the earth, the more weight it has; for example, a car weighs more at sea level than it does on a mountaintop. But the mass remains the same. A body's mass never changes; it is a constant property. Thus a body in space, such as an asteroid, probably

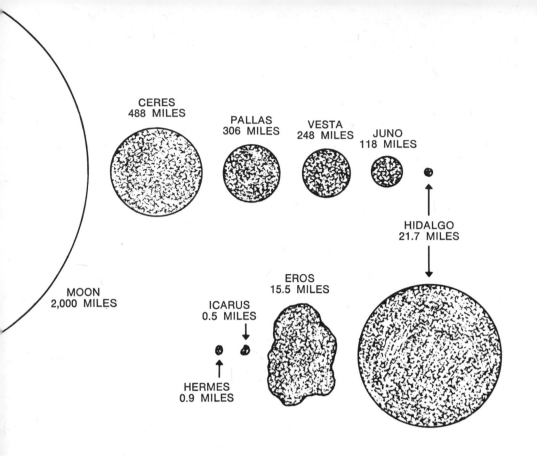

Relative sizes of well-known asteroids.

would have very little or no actual measurable weight, although it does have mass.

It is assumed that the asteroids have an average density comparable to that of the earth's crust or the moon's; thus their mass can be estimated mathematically by multiplying their density by their volume. Astronomers have calculated that the mass of Ceres, the largest asteroid, is probably only about 1/8000 that of the earth. Hence it would have a very small gravitational force and be unable to hold any sort of atmosphere, for the larger the mass of a celestial body, the greater is its gravitational force. On some of the tinier asteroids, the pull of gravity is so weak that a baseball hurled into space would never return. Indeed, it has been calculated that if the combined masses of all the known asteroids plus those only estimated to exist were lumped into one great mass, the whole would amount to only about 1/500 of the earth's.

The smaller asteroids, with a diameter of only a few miles or less, have so little gravity that they cannot even pull themselves into a spherical shape. The four largest asteroids, with a larger mass, have achieved a more or less spherical shape. So, of course, have the nine planets. So great is the gravitational force of these bodies that the material of which they are composed slumps in on itself under its own weight until the outside surface becomes uniformly rounded. But the gravitational force in the average asteroid is so small that once an irregular shape has been assumed, it tends to stay that way.

Because of the asteroids' tiny gravitational pull, an astronaut suddenly transported to one would find himself practically weightless. Even on the largest, Ceres, a man weighing a hundred pounds on earth would weigh only about four pounds. On an asteroid of some ten miles in diameter, the same man would weigh only about an ounce. And, should that same man land on Icarus, whose diameter is less than a mile, he would weigh but a fraction of an ounce.

Surface conditions on the asteroids surely must be bleak and barren. No atmosphere, wind, or water exists to smooth the original jagged surface by weathering and erosion. Even had there once been water on the asteroids, it would have evaporated long ago into space. Likewise, what little heat the asteroids receive from the distant sun must be radiated away. Lacking the protective blanket of earth's atmosphere to hold and absorb such heat, the asteroids must have surface temperatures very near absolute zero, 273 degrees below zero Celsius. At such temperatures, even rudimentary forms of plant or animal life scarcely could survive. However, until men land on the asteroids, this assumption remains uncertain.

Except for its highly eccentric orbit, bringing it close to earth at times, Icarus is probably a typical asteroid. On its close approach to earth in 1968, astronomers observed it by means of radar. The radar reflections indicated that Icarus rotates approximately once every two and a half hours and that it is probably only about a half mile in diameter—not the one mile astronomers had estimated previously. Observers at Cal Tech's Jet Propulsion Laboratory followed the asteroid in seven spaced experiments of about three hours each during a three-day period. While the radar scanners did not tell whether its surface was primarily stoney or metallic, the findings did indicate that Icarus must have a rough, jagged shape instead of the roundish one that had been assumed previously.

As science develops more sophisticated space probes, astronomers will be able to observe the asteroids at closer range and find out still more about their physical nature.

4
THEORIES
OF
ORIGIN

Why are thousands of these tiny planets in orbit about the sun? Where did the asteroids come from?

Most astronomers think that the minor planets probably originated within the solar system. They also believe that the asteroids were formed from the same material that formed the major planets, and at about the same time. How they did so would depend, of course, on how the solar system itself evolved— a riddle scientists are still a long way from solving.

Perhaps, however, clues supplied by greater knowledge of the asteroids will help to provide the solution.

At present a number of theories concerning the origin of the minor planets are being considered:

1. They may have been created by the breakup or disintegration of a larger planet.
2. They may have come from small protoplanets between Mars and Jupiter. The protoplanet hypothesis, proposed by the American astronomer G. P. Kuiper, suggests that great clouds of gaseous matter, the so-called protoplanets, cooled, contracted, and condensed into the present nine major planets. The same process may have taken place on a smaller scale to form the asteroids.
3. They may have been caused by the collision of two larger bodies—perhaps embryonic ones, perhaps solidified ones—producing further fragments.
4. They may be captured bodies from outside the solar system.
5. They may be the product of a ring of matter either surrounding the sun or one formerly associated with Jupiter.

The first three theories—or combinations of them —are considered the most likely by astronomers today. Heinrich Olbers, discoverer of Pallas and Vesta, believed that the asteroids were the result of a catastrophic breakup of a larger body, presumably a planet that once revolved around the sun at 2.8 astronomical units. There are, however, two objections to this hypothesis. First, the mass of all the minor planets is only about one fifth that of our own moon, itself a rather small body. Second, no common point of origin has been found for the asteroids. Yet it has been proved that if such a disruption had taken place, any fragment would have to pass through the original point of disruption each time it orbited the sun, unless the orbit were changed by severe perturbations. Moreover, the possibility of any such common point seems unlikely when one considers the unusual orbits of such asteroids as Hidalgo and Icarus.

There is some evidence that many of the asteroids may have originated from the breakup of parent bodies somewhat larger than the asteroids. In 1917, a Japanese astronomer, Kiyotsugo Hirayama, completed a long and arduous study of asteroidal orbits. He was looking for one common point of origin for the many asteroids he had studied, but instead he announced that he had found *five*. Each of them involved a different group, or family, of asteroids that he identified by the name of the brightest member of the group. They were the Flora family with eight members; the Maria family with thirteen members; the Eos family with twenty-three members; the Koronis family with fifteen members; and the Themis family with twenty-five members. Hirayama theorized that each family may have been produced by a different explosion or by the collision of two bodies. Yet this explanation makes the problem more difficult, since these five exploding planets would have been far smaller than the single exploding planet imagined by Olbers would have been.

More recently some scientists have suggested that the asteroids may come from a planet that was broken up by the gravitational might of Jupiter. However, this argument can be reversed to say that the asteroids are chunks of matter that never united to form a planet when the solar system was created. That Jupiter *has* caused disturbances in the asteroid zone is known, as Kirkwood's gaps bear witness, but whether or not it played a major role in the origin of the minor planets is still uncertain.

In 1950, the Dutch astronomer Dirk Brouwer extended Hirayama's work to the study of over 1500 asteroids and their orbits. Brouwer found that these asteroids could be grouped into twenty-nine families containing from four to sixty-two members. Some of these families could be further subdivided into two more groups, suggesting that such families may have resulted from a collision of two bodies. Brouwer's work thus has helped to reinforce the collision theory, which today is favored by many scientists.

In the opinion of Gerard P. Kuiper, the original theory that a planet broke up to form the asteroids is, with certain modifications, still the best. Such a breakup might be possible in four ways: explosion; too-rapid rotation; tidal disruption in the planet's matter, caused by the close approach of another large body; and collision.

Kuiper dismissed the first three as improbable and perhaps even impossible. The last he felt was the most likely. The collision may have occurred between two small bodies, and a small degree of velocity would be sufficient to cause a breakup. According to Kuiper's theory of the formation of the solar system, some five or ten protoplanets may have existed in the present asteroid belt. A collision between two of them certainly would have been possible.

After the first collision took place, further collisions between fragments would have followed. In this manner, families of asteroids could have come into being. It has been calculated that if such colliding fragments of a larger body had velocities of only .06 to .12 miles per second, the present distribution of the asteroid families could be accounted for. If this collision and fragmentation theory of the asteroids should ever be proved correct, the supposition is that the fragmentation still is going on. In other words, new asteroids would be forming from time to time.

The collision theory also accounts for certain known facts about the tiny planets. Many of them would be, and in fact are, quite irregular in shape, and their orbits would differ greatly in size, shape, and inclination as they do. In addition, many meteoroids have orbits similar to the asteroids' and perhaps may be considered asteroidal debris. The structure of meteorites indicates that they were once fragments of much larger bodies.

A further interesting observation is that short-period comets, those orbiting the sun quickly, have orbits resembling those of some of the more eccentric asteroids. Hence, there is speculation that these two types of bodies have some relation to each other. Perhaps some asteroids may be the remains of comets.

5

PRESENT
AND
FUTURE
USE

Of what possible value to mankind are these seemingly useless lumps of rock endlessly circling our sun? Will they play any future role in the ever-broadening investigation of our solar system?

The fact is that certain asteroids already provide much valuable planetary data. Particularly important are those minor planets that wander in close to the earth, for they can be used to determine the precise value of that yardstick of the solar system—the astronomical unit. Although the distance from the earth to the sun has been known accurately for several years by use of certain radar observations of Venus, astronomers still like to have independent verification of such a measurement.

If the orbit of a typical asteroid has been calculated accurately, its distance from the earth in astronomical units is known at all times. When the same asteroid swings in close to the earth, its distance from us in miles also can be computed. Thus scientists can make a check on the astronomical unit itself. Observations of Eros were made for exactly this purpose in 1931 when that asteroid passed close to earth. Other techniques depending on perturbations of the minor planets also are used to find out the value of the astronomical unit.

In 1968 the most exhaustive study to date was made at the Yale Observatory to determine a precise figure for the astronomical unit. Using more than 8000 observations of Eros taken over a period of more than seventy years, it was calculated that the astronomical unit was 92,957,200 miles, plus or minus 50 miles. This figure agrees almost exactly

Opposite: The apparent path of Eros among the constellations on its near approach to earth in 1931.
Courtesy of the American Museum of Natural History

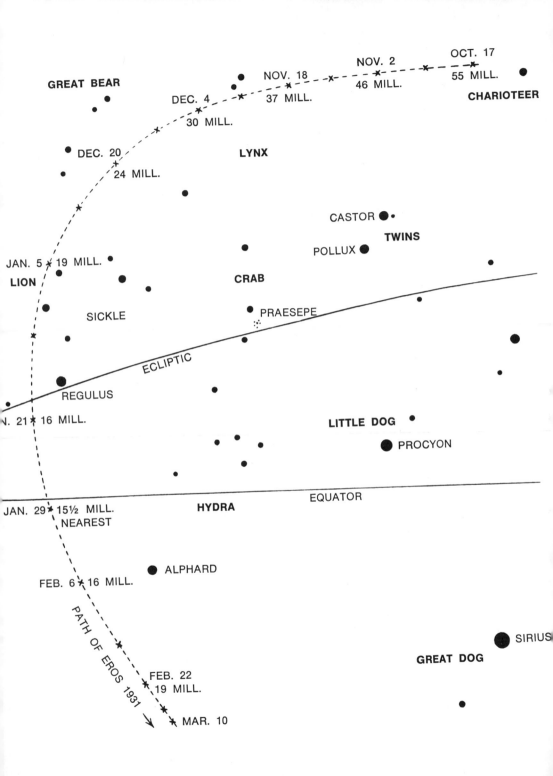

with the figure obtained by radar observations of Venus.

The asteroids also provide a means of determining the masses of the major planets, our own moon, and even other asteroids. This information is obtained by observing and measuring how much the orbit of an asteroid is perturbed by the gravitational attraction of the earth, Venus, the moon, or whatever larger body the asteroid passes near. So small is the asteroid in comparison to the larger body that its orbital motion is changed, giving astronomers figures that can be used in the calculation of the larger body's mass. For example, in 1968, scientists at the Goddard Space Center used the perturbations in the orbit of the minor planet Areta to compute the mass of Vesta, the third largest asteroid, which was found to be 200 million billion metric tons.

The fact that the smallness of the asteroids makes them so sensitive to perturbations by bigger bodies has opened up a whole new field of research for astronomers. In 1972, two scientists, one working in the United States and the other in Sweden, published a study of Toro, an irregularly shaped asteroid.

Toro is about a mile and a half long and a mile wide and has an eccentric orbit. The results of the study revealed that apparently, over many centuries, the earth and Venus have been "tossing" Toro back and forth between them like a giant tennis ball. With the aid of computers, the two astronomers were able to go back 1000 years into Toro's history and chart its complicated orbital motion.

The study showed that Toro's orbit has been perturbed by earth for a number of centuries, then by Venus for a number of centuries. At present, earth controls the asteroid, but eventually the gravitational force of earth will send it under the gravitational influence of Venus again. The study shows that earth has controlled Toro's orbital path since the year 1580. In the year 2200, Venus will become dominant; in the year 2350, earth will again control; in the year 2800, Venus will command once more.

The tiny planets have demonstrated their usefulness to mankind in other ways as well. They have stimulated international cooperation among astronomers, as in the case of the work on Toro. They have presented interesting problems in celestial me-

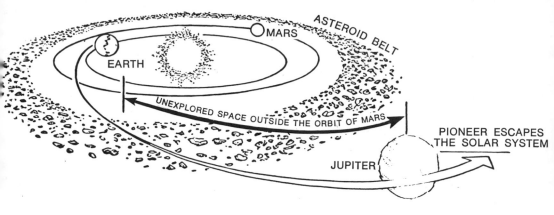

The sketch shows Pioneer 10 passing the orbit of Mars, traversing the asteroid belt, passing Jupiter, and escaping from the solar system. *NASA*

chanics. Asteroids also have been used to measure the solar parallax, which is a measure of the distance of the earth from the sun, and like the astronomical unit, an important yardstick in astronomy.

The subject of asteroids is everywhere receiving increased attention. Several of the larger American observatories have been carrying out extensive programs for observing the minor planets, while much theoretical work is being done at the Cincinnati, Berkeley, and Yale observatories. In Europe, the Astronomisches Rechen Institut of Heidelberg, Germany, and the Academy of Sciences in the Soviet Union published data on an immense number of asteroidal orbits and their perturbations. Excellent research is taking place at other European observatories, in Japan, and in the Republic of South Africa.

Eventually we shall wish to send out a spacecraft to photograph the asteroids to see what they really look like. In the meantime, the American space program has launched the Pioneer 10 probe toward Jupiter to find out more about this largest planet of

An artist's conception of Pioneer 10 over Jupiter's surface.
NASA

our solar system. On its way there the spacecraft passed successfully through the thickly populated asteroid belt.

In the farther future, earthmen surely will visit the tiny planets, as they have the moon already. Except for the almost nonexistent gravity on the smaller asteroids, conditions will not be unlike those encountered on the moon. There will be no atmosphere, no air to breathe. Men must bring their air with them, probably strapped to their backs like the moon-walking astronauts of today. They will stare out on bleak, jagged terrains with a sharp horizon line dividing the faintly sunlit surface from the inky blackness of interplanetary space. To prevent themselves from drifting off into space, their spacesuits will have to be equipped with heavy weights or other compensatory devices, and they probably will have to rig lifelines to walk about in safety. The mother ship that brings them there will have to be anchored securely to the asteroid's surface.

If men choose to visit one of the asteroids of the Trojan group, they will see wondrously strange sights. The immense planet Jupiter, with its mysteri-

Opposite: An artist's conception of the probable landscape on the asteroid Eros. Drawing by Scriven Bolton.
Courtesy of the American Museum of Natural History

ous Great Red Spot, will loom almost perpetually in the sky. Saturn with its rings probably will be visible. Mars, Venus, and the earth will be seen to change their positions in the heavens like so many evening stars. Companion asteroids may appear as fixed moons, either leading or trailing the earthmen's asteroid, locked in their lonely orbits around the distant sun by the powerful grip of Jupiter's gravity. And the sun itself will glow faintly at the center of all, smaller and less brilliant to the earthmen's eyes than it appears from their native planet.

Perhaps the earthmen's first visit will be to such small, relatively nearby asteroids as Hermes or Icarus or Apollo, tiny planets only about a mile in diameter. Their visit will have to be a short one, for the asteroid will swing away quickly far into space.

Or perhaps an asteroid passing close to earth will be earmarked for other purposes. Conceivably earthmen may want to capture an asteroid for a ready-made space station someday. By diverting the asteroid out of its orbit with a rocket engine—or a series of them—attached to its surface, the tiny planet could be pushed off course and eventually guided into a convenient earth orbit. Then the asteroid could be converted into the desired vehicle for harboring scientists, laboratories, and equipment.

Certainly an asteroid, once landed on by men, could be employed for installing telescopes, cameras, lasers, and other scientific equipment—all remotely controlled from earth or elsewhere. Earthmen need not stay on the asteroid permanently but may return from time to time to check and service equipment or to refuel and rest there while on other missions in the solar system. Perhaps there even will be permanent colonies established on the larger asteroids.

There is no limit to the possibilities that beckon the imagination, and as astronomers continue to gather and add to the known facts about the minor planets, those possibilities come closer and closer to the realm of reality.

TABLE OF PHYSICAL AND ORBITAL DATA
FOR SOME OF THE ASTEROIDS

Catalog Number and Name	Year of Discovery	Orbital Period (in earth years)	Diameter (miles)	Eccentricity	Degree of Inclination of Orbit to Earth's
(1) Ceres	1801	4.6	488	.08	10.6
(2) Pallas	1802	4.6	306	.24	34.82
(3) Juno	1804	4.3	118	.26	13.02
(4) Vesta	1807	3.6	248	.09	7.14
(5) Astraea	1845	4.1	50	.18	5.33
(6) Hebe	1847	3.7	70	.2	11.65
(7) Iris	1847	3.7	77	.23	5.47
(8) Flora	1847	3.2	56	.15	5.88
(9) Metis	1848	3.7	77	.12	5.6
(12) Victoria	1850	3.5	37	.22	8.38

(15)	Melpomene	1852	3.5	59	.21	10.15
(20)	Massalia	1852	3.7	66	.14	.68
(192)	Nausicaa	1879	3.7	46	.24	6.87
(324)	Bamberga	1892	4.4	59	.33	11.3
(387)	Aquitania	1894	4.5	66	.23	17.97
(433)	Eros	1898	1.7	15.5	.22	10.8
(719)	Albert	1911	4.1	2.5	.54	10.82
(944)	Hidalgo	1920	13.7	21.7	.65	43.06
(1036)	Ganymede	1924	4.3	?	.54	23.2
(1221)	Amor	1932	2.7	1.6	.45	?
—	Apollo	1932	1.8	1.2	.56	6.4
—	Adonis	1936	2.7	.6	.78	1.5
—	Hermes	1937	1.4	.9	.47	4.7
(1566)	Icarus	1949	1.1	.5	.79	21.

GLOSSARY

albedo: the percentage of sunlight that a planet or minor planet reflects from its surface

aphelion: the point in a planet's orbit where it is farthest from the sun

asteroid: one of tens of thousands of small planets ranging in size from a few hundred miles to less than a mile in diameter; also called a minor planet or planetoid

asteroid belt: the zone between Mars and Jupiter where the asteroids are most numerous

astronomical unit (AU): a yardstick for distances within the solar system equal to the mean distance of the earth from the sun; approximately 93 million miles *atmosphere:* the gaseous envelope surrounding a celestial body

celestial body: a general term for all objects that can be observed in the sky beyond the earth's atmosphere: the sun, the moon, the planets and their satellites, comets, stars, etc.; a heavenly body

celestial mechanics: the branch of astronomy that deals with the motions of celestial bodies under the forces of gravitation; also called gravitational astronomy

comet: a swarm of solid particles and gases that revolves around the sun, usually in an orbit of high eccentricity

constellation: a configuration of stars named for a particular object, person, or animal, such as the Great Bear; the area of the sky assigned to a particular configuration

density: the amount of matter in a unit volume of substance

eccentricity: the degree of flattening of an ellipse, its deviation from a circular shape

ecliptic: the plane of the earth's orbit around the sun

ellipse: a plane curve on which the sum of the distances from any point of its circumference to two points within, called the foci, is always the same

gravitation: the force of attraction that exists among all particles of matter everywhere in the universe

inclination (of an orbit): the angle between the orbital plane of a revolving body, such as an asteroid, and the plane of the earth's orbit

Kirkwood's gaps: gaps, or vacancies, in the spacing of the asteroids' distances from the sun

major planet: one of the nine principal planets of the solar system

mass: a measure of the total amount of matter that a body contains *minor planet:* see *asteroid*

moon: in general, a satellite; specifically, the satellite of the earth; see *satellite*

orbit: the path of a body that is in revolution about another body, as an asteroid about the sun

perihelion: the point in a planet's orbit where it is closest to the center of the sun

period: in the solar system, the time required for a celestial body, such as a planet or asteroid, to make one revolution about the sun; also, the time required for a satellite to make one revolution around its primary body, as the moon about the earth; a celestial body's "year"

perturbation: the deviation of a planet or other celestial body from its normal orbital path owing to the gravitational effect of another body or bodies

photometer: an astronomical instrument for measuring the intensity of light from a source such as a star or a planet

planetoid: see *asteroid*

protoplanet: the original gaseous material from which the embryonic planets cooled, contracted, and solidified into the present planets; a planet in its early formative stage

radar: from *r*adio *d*etection *a*nd *r*anging; a technique for determining distance by observing the reflection of radio waves from a distant object like a star or planet

retrograde motion: an apparent backward, or counterclockwise, motion of a planet among the stars

rotational period: the time required for a planet or similar body to turn once on its axis; its "day"

satellite: a body that revolves around a larger one, as a moon of a planet

solar parallax: the angular size of the earth's radius as it would theoretically be measured from the center of the sun, or one astronomical unit away

solar system: the system of the sun and its planets, their satellites, the minor planets, comets, and other objects revolving around the sun

star: an immense glowing sphere of gas so far from the solar system that it appears only as a point of light; a sun. Unlike the planets, a star shines by its own light, which is produced by nuclear reactions within it

sun: the star about which the earth and other planets revolve; see *star*

INDEX

indicates illustrations

Born in Glens Falls, New York, David C. Knight received his education both in this country and abroad. After earning his BA degree at Union College, Schenectady, New York, he spent a year at the Sorbonne, in Paris, then continued his studies at the Engineering Institute, in Philadelphia, and at the University of Pennsylvania.

After serving in the U.S. Army during World War II, Mr. Knight worked as an editor and production man with Prentice-Hall. Later he became senior science editor at Franklin Watts, the position he holds today. Science has been one of Mr. Knight's major interests, and he has written twenty-six books on various scientific subjects. He also has written a number of science articles for the *New Book of Knowledge*.

At present Mr. Knight lives in Dobbs Ferry, N.Y., with his wife and two daughters.